Kids' Travel Guide
Rome

FlyingKids Presents:
Kids' Travel Guide
Rome

Authors: Elisa Davoglio & Shiela H. Leon

Editor: Carma Graber

Graphic Designer: Neboysha Dolovacki

Cover Illustrations and design: Francesca Guido

Visit us @ www.theflyingkids.com

Contact us: leonardo@theflyingkids.com

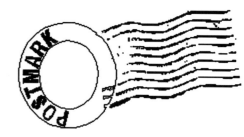

ISBN: 978-1499677812

Acknowledgement:
All images are from Diomedia and public domain except those mentioned below:
Canstockphoto: 13m, 20mc, 22mt, 35mb; Dreamstime: 17mt;
Shutterstock: 10bg, 11-19bg, 21mt, 21mc, 21mb, 27mb;
Attribution: 10bg to 19bg-© Tripomatic, 2014. Built using data from Tripomatic, CloudMade and OpenStreetMap.org contributors; 22mb- "RomaForoRomanoMiliariumAureum" by MM, 24mb- By Jaakko Luttinen (Own work) [CC BY-SA 3.0 (http://creativecommons.org/licenses/by-sa/3.0)], via Wikimedia.

Key: t=top; b=bottom; l=left; r=right, c=center; m=main image; bg=background

Table of Contents

This is the only page for parents in this book...

Dear Parents,

If you bought this book, you're probably planning a family trip with your kids. You are spending a lot of time and money in the hopes that this family vacation will be pleasant and fun. Of course, you would be happy for your children to get to know the city to which you are traveling — a little of its geography, a little local history, important sites, culture, customs, and more. And you hope they will always remember the trip as a very special experience.

The reality is often quite different. Parents find themselves frustrated as they struggle to convince their kids to join a tour or visit a landmark, while the kids just want to stay in and watch TV, or they are glued to their mobile devices instead of enjoying the new sights and scenery." Many parents are disappointed when they return home and discover that their kids don't remember much about the trip and the new things they learned.

That's exactly why the Kids' Travel Guides were created.

With the Kids' Travel Guides, young children become researchers and active participants in the trip. During the vacation, kids will read relevant facts about the city you are visiting. The Kids' Travel Guides include puzzles, tasks to complete, useful tips, and other recommendations along the way. The kids will meet Leonardo — their tour guide. Leonardo encourages them to experiment, explore, and be more involved in the family's activities — as well as to learn new information and make memories throughout the trip. In addition, kids are encouraged to document and write about their experiences during the trip, so that when you return home, they will have a memoir that will be fun to look at and reread again and again.

The Kids' Travel Guides support children as they get ready for the trip, visit new places, learn new things, and finally, return home.

The Kids' Travel Guide — Rome focuses on the Eternal City. In it, children will find background information on Rome and its special attractions. The Kids' Travel Guide — Rome focuses on central sites that are recommended for children. At each of these sites, interesting facts, action items, and quizzes, await your kids. You, the parents, are invited to participate or to find an available bench and relax while you enjoy your active children.

If you are traveling to Italy, you may also want to get the Kids' Travel Guide — Italy. It focuses on the country of Italy — its geography, history, unique culture, traditions, and more — using the fun and interesting style of the Kids' Travel Guide series.

Hi, Kids!

If you are reading this book, it means you are lucky — you are going to **Rome**!

You may have noticed that your parents are getting ready for the journey. They have bought travel guides, looked for information on the Internet, and printed pages of information. They are talking to friends and people who have already visited Rome in order to learn about it and know what to do, where to go, and when … But this is not just another guidebook for your parents.

This book is for you only — the young traveler.

So what is this book all about?

First and foremost, meet **Leonardo**, your very own personal guide on this trip. Leonardo has visited **many places** around the world (guess how he got there?), and he will be with you throughout the book and the trip. Leonardo will tell you all about the places you will visit … It is always good to learn a little bit about the place and its history beforehand. He will give you many ideas, quizzes, tips, and other surprises. Leonardo will accompany you while you are packing and leaving home. He will stay in the hotel with you. (Don't worry — it doesn't cost more money!) And he will see the sights with you until you return home.

Going to Rome!!!

How did you get to Rome?

By plane / train / car / other _____ _plane_

Date of arrival _Sunday_ Time _8:00_ Date of departure _____

All in all, we will stay in **Rome** for ____ _4_ ____ days.

Is this your first visit ____ _yes_ ____ ?

Where will you sleep? In a (hotel) / in a campsite / in an apartment / (other)

What sites are you planning to visit?

_____

_____

_____

What special activities are you planning to do?

_____

_____

_____

Are you excited about the trip?

This is an excitement indicator. Ask your family members how excited they are (from "not at all" up to "very, very much"), and mark each of their answers on the indicator. Leonardo has already marked the level of his excitement …

not at all   very, very much

|————————————————————————|

Leonardo

Who is
traveling?

Write down the names of the family members traveling with you and their answers to the questions.

Paste a picture of your family.

Name: _____

Age: _____

Has he or she visited Rome before? yes / no

What is the most exciting thing about your upcoming trip?

_____
_____
_____

Name: _____

Age: _____

Has he or she visited Rome before? yes / no

What is the most exciting thing about your upcoming trip?

_____
_____
_____

Name: _____

Age: _____

Has he or she visited Rome before? yes / no

What is the most exciting thing about your upcoming trip?

_____
_____
_____

Name: _____

Age: _____

Has he or she visited Rome before? yes / no

What is the most exciting thing about your upcoming trip?

_____
_____
_____

Name: _____

Age: _____

Has he or she visited Rome before? yes / no

What is the most exciting thing about your upcoming trip?

_____
_____
_____

Preparations at home — DO NOT FORGET ...!

Mom or Dad will take care of packing clothes (how many pairs of pants, which comb to take …). So Leonardo will only tell you about the stuff he thinks you may want to bring along to Rome.

Here's the **Packing List** Leonardo made for you. You can check off each item as you pack it:

- ☐ *Kids' Travel Guide — Rome* — of course!
- ☐ Comfortable walking shoes
- ☐ A raincoat (One that folds up is best — sometimes it rains without warning …)
- ☐ A hat (and sunglasses, if you want)
- ☐ Pens and pencils
- ☐ Crayons and markers (It is always nice to color and paint.)
- ☐ A notebook or a writing pad (You can use it for games or writing, or to draw or doodle in when you're bored …)
- ☐ A book to read
- ☐ Your smartphone/tablet or camera
- ☐ _____
- ☐ _____

Pack your things in a small bag (or **backpack**). You may also want to take these things:

Snacks, fruit, candy, and chewing gum. If you are flying, it can help a lot during takeoff and landing when there's pressure in your ears.

Some games you can play while sitting down: electronic games, booklets of crossword puzzles, connect-the-numbers, etc.

Now let's see if you can find 12 items you should take on a trip in this word search puzzle:

- Leonardo ✓
- walking shoes
- hat ✓ hat
- raincoat
- crayons
- book ✓
- pencil
- camera ✓
- snacks ✓
- fruit
- patience
- good mood ✓

P	A	T	I	E	N	C	E	A	W	F	G
E	L	R	T	S	G	Y	J	W	A	T	O
Q	B	Y	U	Y	K	Z	K	M	L	W	O
H	O	S	N	A	S	N	Y	S	K	G	D
A	N	R	Z	C	P	E	N	C	I	L	M
C	A	M	E	R	A	A	W	G	N	E	O
R	R	A	I	N	C	O	A	T	G	Q	O
Y	D	S	G	I	R	K	Z	K	S	H	D
S	C	A	C	O	A	E	T	K	H	A	T
F	R	U	I	T	Y	Q	O	V	O	D	A
B	O	O	K	F	O	H	Z	K	E	R	T
T	K	Z	K	A	N	S	I	E	S	Y	U
O	V	I	E	S	S	N	A	C	K	S	P

Welcome to Rome, the Eternal City

Welcome to Rome, one of the world's most beautiful and fascinating cities! Rome is the capital of Italy. It's called the "Eternal City" because of its long life … over 2,500 years!

There is a lot to see … ready? You'll come across majestic ruins, awe-inspiring monuments, and amazing art! And it will be a thrill to discover the power of the ancient Roman Empire, because it had such a big influence on the world you live in today.

Why is Rome called Rome?

Romulus and his twin brother, Remus, were the children of a princess named Rhea Silvia and Mars, the god of war. Their greedy great-uncle abandoned them by the River Tiber, but a female wolf rescued them and fed them with her milk. When they grew up, they decided to build a city on the spot where the she-wolf had found them. But they had a fight about where it should be. Romulus killed Remus and then built the city, naming it after himself.

When you visit Rome, you will find these letters after the dates on monuments: **"AD"** and **"BC."** What do they mean?
AD is AFTER Jesus was born; BC is BEFORE Jesus was born.

Leonardo knows that the birth of Rome happened in 753 BC. How old was Rome in 2015?
- ◆ 753 years
- ◆ 1,753 years
- ◆ 2,768 years

Answer: 2,768

Write your date of birth:

I was born _____ AD/BC!

Did you know?

This statue is the symbol of Rome. It shows a wolf feeding the twins Romulus and Remus. It's called the **"Capitoline Wolf"** because it's located in the Capitoline Museum on the ancient Capitoline Hill.

What does Rome look like?

Rome was built on seven hills. These hills are the oldest part of the city, and the most visited. You'll find a lot of the monuments there.

A long river crosses the city and then divides into two parts. It flows under many beautiful bridges, and it even has a little island. Do you know the name of this river? You can take a look at the map for a clue ... 😉

Quizzes! What is the name of the island that sits in the river?

Did you know?

Inside the city of Rome, there is a separate, independent country: the Vatican! This country is governed by the Pope and the Holy Catholic Church.

It's also the smallest country in the world. Only 800 people live there! 😉

Can you help Leonardo find all seven hills in Rome?

- Aventine Hill
- Caelian Hill
- Capitoline Hill
- Esquiline Hill
- Palatine Hill
- Quirinal Hill
- Viminal Hill

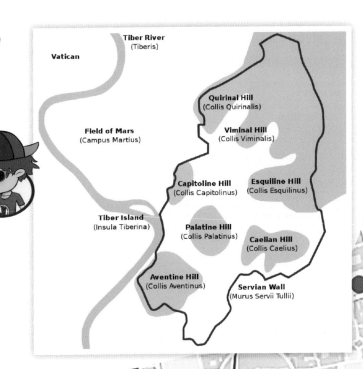

Answer: Tiber

Answer: Tiber Island

Things to see only in Rome!

Rome is the ideal place to wander around. It's an amazing space where you can touch really ancient times — and feel like an ancient gladiator! So let's go ... There is so much to see in Rome! But don't worry — Leonardo will tell you about all the things you don't want to miss!

Here are a few fun things to do in Rome:

- **Throw a coin into the Trevi Fountain: Make a wish, and then use your right hand to toss the coin over your left shoulder. Remember — your back has to be to the fountain if you want your wish to come true!**

- **Visit the Colosseum, one of the Seven Wonders of the World! You'll be impressed by the greatness of the place where ancient gladiators fought.**

- **Enjoy fantastic views of ancient monuments, and imagine yourself as a powerful and triumphant emperor.**

- **Taste Italian ice cream (called "gelato") or a slice of pizza during your walks ... There are so many different kinds of food in Italy that Leonardo hasn't finished discovering them all yet!**

- **Try to speak in Italian by learning some famous Italian words, such as:**

Ciao! = Hello!

Help Leonardo pronounce some Italian phrases:

- *Per favore* → sounds like: **pear fa-vor-reh** *(Can I have...)*
- *Buon giorno* → sounds like: **bwon zhor-no** *(Good morning)*
- *Buona sera* → sounds like: **bwoh-nah say-rah** *(Good evening)*
- *Grazie* → sounds like: **graht-zee-ay** *(Thank you)*

Rome's special language — symbols and signs ...

There are a lot of symbols (lions, dragons, stars, trees, and many others) carved into all the monuments in Rome.

Every symbol has its special meaning! But they were all created to show the power of the Roman Empire and its victories and superiority.

The most famous slogan in Rome!

You'll find this slogan all over the city.
The letters *SPQR* mean *Senatus Populusque Romanus* in Latin, or "the Senate and the people of Rome."

Quizzes!

What was the animal symbol for military power in Rome?

Panther
Eagle
Lion
Wolf
Boar

Answer: Eagle

Did you know?

What kind of crown did the **emperor wear**?
Not a crown made of gold or silver or precious gems! The emperor wore a crown of laurel leaves, a symbol of the highest honor!

Find a laurel plant and build your own **crown**!
Now people will think that You are a very important person! ⌣

PIGNA

VIA DEL CORSO

The ROMAN EMPIRE — a great history!

Have you heard the saying *"Rome wasn't built in a day"*? … Well, its long life is an amazing story!

Around 750 BC, Rome was a little village on the River Tiber that was ruled by the Etruscans (people from the center of Italy). But after about 250 years, a revolt against King Tarquin the Proud ended the power of the Etruscans, and Rome became a republic.

The Roman Republic was the most powerful city in the Mediterranean area. It spread its practices and its example of democracy to others.
Julius Caesar was the last leader of the republic. After his death, the new leader, **Octavian Augustus**, was called the emperor, and the Roman Empire began. It was the biggest empire in the world for over four centuries. Its power extended everywhere.

This is a statue of the first emperor of Rome, **Augustus**.
Pay attention to the pose of the emperor:
You'll see many Roman statues in this position.
The right arm is raised to show the authority and power of the person.

Try to find at least one statue with this pose in Rome …
Where did you find it?

_____

_____

 If you save pictures of all the statues you see in this pose, you'll create a collection of Roman emperors!

The fall of Rome and the power of the POPES

The Roman Empire began to get weaker when the Barbarians attacked.

Have you ever heard of the Barbarians?

They were tribes of people living outside the Roman Empire. They didn't speak Latin, and the Romans thought their language sounded like "bar-bar-bar." That's why the Romans called them "barbarians."

In the **medieval period,*** Rome lost its power. But during the Renaissance, the Catholic Popes wanted to make Rome important again. So they decided to fill the city with magnificent new monuments. These monuments were built to show the Pope's power and the superiority of the Catholic Church.

Did you know?

*The medieval period, or Middle Ages, started with the fall of the Roman Empire around 400 AD. It ended with the **Renaissance (a French word that means "rebirth"). As its name says, the Renaissance period was a time of rebirth** for knowledge, with new discoveries in art and science.

The city of Rome was part of the Catholic Church until 1870. That's when **Rome became the capital of Italy, which it still is today!**

Do you know the name of the current Pope?

Quizzes!

_____

Where does he live? _____

Answer: Pope Francis
He lives in Vatican City.

PIGNA

VIA DEL CORSO

Let's go! How to get around in Rome

Use your feet … Walking in Rome is a wonderful experience, since amazing monuments and beautiful buildings are all around …

Tip! No matter what kind of transportation you and your family choose, Leonardo wants to remind you that **Rome is built on seven hills**. So make sure you have comfortable shoes to wear!

Option #1

The easiest and fastest way to get around in Rome is the subway. It gets you to all the major attractions easily. There are two lines: Line **A**, the red line, and Line B, the blue line. Their entrances are shown by a large red sign marked with an **M**.

Tip! You can tell your parents that if you are under age 10, you don't need to pay a fare — you can travel free with an adult!

Use this map to help your family organize your route!
The subway lines make a rough X.

Leonardo visited the Colosseum, and now he wants to go to the Spanish Steps (Spagna). **Can you** help him plan his route using the subway? What is the color of the line he's on now? How many stations is it to the Spanish Steps?

Answer: To reach the Spanish Steps — Spagna — Leonardo has to take the blue line to Termini (central station), and then the red line for three stops.

Option #2

The other way to travel around Rome is by **bus**. There are many routes available, but buses are often very crowded.

The most popular bus line is 40 Express. It connects the center of Rome to the Vatican and St. Peter's Square. **Don't expect an orderly line!**

Option #3

You can also get on a **tourist bus**. The **110 OPEN is a special double-decker red bus** that goes to some of the most famous sights — like the Colosseum, Piazza Navona, and St. Peter's Square.

This bus lets you **hop on and hop off** at any of the stops for the whole day.

You'll get wonderful photos and video from the OPEN Bus!

There is another way to travel in Rome — by horse-drawn carriage! Have you ever taken a carriage ride?

How would you most like to get around in Rome? _____

Which kind of transportation is your family going to use in Rome?

_____

It's time to eat in Rome!

Have you heard about Italian food? Well ... Leonardo has a lot of fantastic foods to tell you about!

Do you like pizza? Pasta? Ice cream? Let's go ...

Who wants ice cream??

Ice cream is called *gelato* in Italian ... Rome is famous for its gelato. You'll find all kinds of different flavors and colors to try. Fortunately, there are many gelato stores (*gelateria* in Italian), so you'll have plenty of chances to taste this special treat!

What are your favorite ice cream flavors?

_____

_____

Who wants pizza?

What kind of pizza do you like? Pizza is one of the most famous foods in the world, and it's very popular in Italy. There are lots of places to get a slice of pizza!

The most common type of pizza is Margherita pizza. It has the three colors of the Italian flag: red — tomatoes, white — mozzarella cheese, and green — basil. Can you see them?

Did you know?

The Margherita pizza was created by pizza maker Raffaele Esposito in 1880 to honor the Queen of Italy, Margherita.

The whole city in your hands!

Would you like to see the whole city from one spot?
Well ... it's possible! Rome has lots of places to visit, but if you want to see it all at once, ask your family to go to one of these high places where you can view the entire city!

Janiculum Hill — hear the cannon go off at noon!
On this green hill high above the Vatican, you can admire a beautiful view of Rome. Every day at noon, a soldier fires a cannon to announce that it's midday.

Vittoriano Monument
Go to the terrace on the roof of the huge Vittoriano Complex. You'll be able to see the whole spectacular landscape of Rome! (Vittoriano Complex is near the ancient Forum in Venezia Square.)

Did you know?
Vittoriano Monument was built to honor Victor Emanuel, the first King of Italy. Find the statue of him on his horse!

Dome of St. Peter
From the beautiful dome of St. Peter's Basilica you can enjoy a 360° view of Rome. Try to find the River Tiber crossing Rome!

See whether you can recognize the Colosseum and other sights from the viewpoints you visit!

In Rome, there are many churches with domes ... How many domes can you count from every viewpoint?

- Two
- More than four
- Less than ten
- More than ten
- Between three and twelve

The ROMAN FORUM: imagine you were ...

The Roman Forum was the heart and soul of ancient Rome. It was the public square where Romans did their banking, trading, shopping, chatting, and praying ... Today, it is a huge archeological* site. The remains are called "ruins." Here you can see what's left of Rome's great past! Let's go discover it!

*Archeologists study the remains of ancient buildings and objects.

Did you know?
Forum is a Latin word meaning "open space" or "marketplace."

Let's start with the main road! Can you recognize it?
A clue ... it begins at an arch ...

The main road of the Forum is called **the Sacred Way** (or *Via Sacra*). **It begins at the Arch of Titus.** This arch was built in 80 AD to celebrate the victories of Emperor Titus against the Jews in Israel.

Did you know?
Arches were built to remember the most important victories and to honor the emperors ... The big battles were fought far away from Rome. When the victorious emperor returned, huge celebrations were held in the Forum!

On the Via Sacra, you'll find another large arch built for an emperor ...
The Arch of Septimius Severus!

Notice the differences between these arches!

Which arch is bigger? _____

What can you read above both arches? _____

Which one is the most ancient? _____

Exploring **the Forum ...**

Stand with your back to the Septimius Severus Arch and your face toward the main road. What do you see on the left? Do you see the big building with three windows above the door?

This brick building is the **Curia** or **Senate House.** The leaders of ancient Rome met here to make decisions about governing the city. The Curia was built by Julius Caesar. In the seventh century AD, the Curia was turned into a church. Many other monuments in the Forum became churches too.

Find another monument in the Forum that was made into a church! Leonardo has a clue: you can count **10 columns** in front of the church!

Next to the Curia is **the Rostra.** On this half-circle platform, the great Roman orators (public speakers) gave their speeches. Crowds of people gathered to listen. Leonardo wants you to pretend you are Julius Caesar and make a speech from the Rostra!

You can announce to your family all your plans for tomorrow: you will wake up at _____ o'clock, and you'll eat a gelato with

Who is Julius Caesar?

Julius Caesar was a famous Roman leader. He was the last consul of Rome before the Roman Empire began. He won many battles and conquered lots of territory to make Rome more powerful. He was the first person to have his head put on a Roman coin.

Answer: The Temple of Antonio and Faustina, now the Chruch of San Lorenzo in Miranda, is located near the ruins of the Basilica Aemilia.
See the map on page 22!

THE TEMPLES — places of power and gods

In ancient Rome, people believed in many gods. They built magnificent temples to thank the gods. The people hoped this would bring them protection and luck.

Near the Rostra, you'll see one of the oldest and most sacred places in Rome — the giant Temple of Saturn. The Roman State Treasury was inside. It stored bronze, silver, and gold. (Find the picture on the next page.)

Quizzes!

How many columns does the Temple of Saturn have?

10

5

8

Look at this picture: it's the **Temple of Vesta**. Here the Vestal Virgins (priestesses) tended a sacred fire so the flame would never go out. Each Vestal Virgin was picked when she was between 6 and 10 years old. They had to serve and remain virgins for 30 years. After that, they could get married. Vestal Virgins were very honored. They had rights that other women didn't.

Try to find the Temple of Vesta! Leonardo has a clue … It is semi-circular, and it's near the Temple of Castor and Pollux, which has only three pillars still remaining …

Who were Castor and Pollux?

They were mythological twin brothers. A legend says they helped Rome defeat the Etruscan King Tarquinius Superbus. Their temple was built at the spot in the Forum where the victory was announced.

Did you know?

In 20 BC, Emperor Augustus built a tall column — called the **Milliarium Aureum** — in front of the Temple of Saturn. The distance to every place in the Roman Empire was measured by starting at this column. Try to find its remains!

Do you know how far it is from your country or your city to Rome?

Who were the *gods* of ancient Rome?

Well, there were a lot of them! Do you know how many gods the ancient Romans worshipped?

- More than 20
- Less than 76
- More than 300

Answer: More than 300

The Romans took many of their gods from the Greeks. They just changed their names. Roman gods were a lot like humans. But the gods had special powers, and they were immortal. They had families and special personalities. They could be moody or cruel or loving. People believed the gods took care of and protected those who honored them.

Who was the king of all the gods? A clue: it's also the biggest **planet** in our solar system!

- Jupiter
- Romulus
- The Pope

Answer: Jupiter

Did you know?
In ancient Rome, it was possible for a person to become a god. Many emperors and members of their families were turned into gods.

Juno was Jupiter's sister and also his wife!
She was the queen of the gods. Juno protected Roman women.

On page 33, you'll find the temple dedicated to all the Roman gods!

Visiting the COLOSSEUM ...
remembering the age of gladiators

The Colosseum is more than 2,000 years old, but it is still one of the most important monuments in the world. It was built by Emperor Vespasian, who was the emperor after Nero.

Nero was one of the most famous emperors in the history of Rome — but not for good reasons! He used his power to build himself a palace, called the Golden House (or *Domus Aurea*). But Emperor Vespasian preferred to build a monument that could hold up to 70,000 spectators. (It was like a modern football stadium!) In the Colosseum, the ancient Romans could be entertained by huge events!

Quizzes!

Try to guess: what was the best way to entertain the ancient Romans?
- A-videogames
- B-television and Internet
- C-musicals and shows
- D-fights between two men or animals

Answer: D- fights between two men or animals

The events at the Colosseum were like deadly reality shows. Gladiators fought each other or wild and angry animals.

Quizzes!

What's the name of a famous emperor who liked to fight as a gladiator?
- A-Arnold Schwarzenegger
- B-Sylvester Stallone
- C-Commodus
- D-Indiana Jones

Answer: C- Emperor Commodus. The movie *The Gladiator* was based on him.

In case you wondered, here is how the Colosseum looked when it was built ...

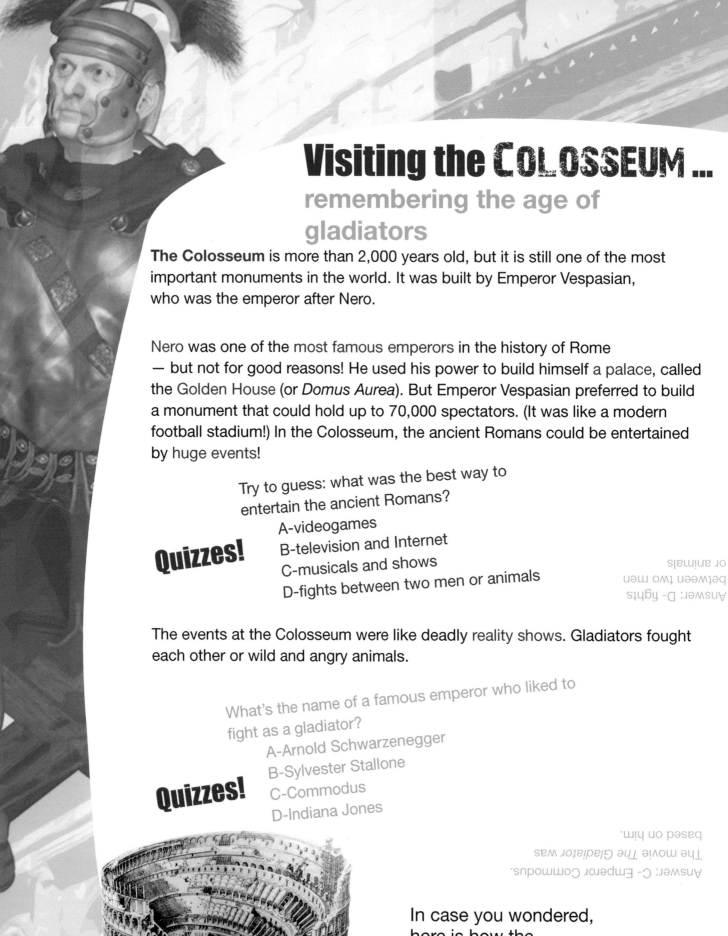

24

What was the life of a GLADIATOR like?

Who were the gladiators?

Gladiators were the professional fighters of ancient Rome. They were often criminals or slaves. Even though they weren't free, they could become famous — just like sports stars today. Gladiators were forced to fight. They lived in a special school close to the Colosseum, where they trained constantly. You have probably seen some movies about gladiators ...

Did you know?
"Gladiator" comes from the Latin word *gladius*, which means "sword."

And what happened when a gladiator wanted to stop fighting?
After losing a fight, the gladiator's life depended on a vote by the crowd — thumbs up or thumbs down.

Did you know?
Most gladiators were men, but there were some women fighters too.

Quizzes!

There were different types of Roman gladiators, and each group had different gear and weapons. Find your gladiator ... Circle the letter that describes the gladiator in the picture!

A-Mirmillo: People called me "fish man" because my helmet was usually decorated with a fish design.

B-Secutor: I wear a helmet with two small, round eye holes.

C-Thracian: I fought with a curved sword and strong body armor.

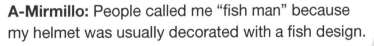

Answer: A-Mirmillo

Discovering the secrets of the Colosseum!

The Colosseum is full of underground passages called **hypogeum**. Here, the animals and gladiators waited under the floor. They were brought up to the arena by special devices. These were designed so the gladiators could come charging out of trapdoors and surprise the people.

Where did the name Colosseum come from?
It's original name was *Amphitheatrum Flavium*. **But it probably became known as** the Colosseum because it was near a giant statue of Nero called *Colosso*.

People could go to the Colosseum **for free**. They were given **cards with numbers** that told them where to sit. If you look above the Colosseum's remaining arches, you can still see the **numbers that matched the cards**.

Did you know?
In ancient Rome, numbers were written as letters of the alphabet!

What numbers match the following Roman numerals?

XXII
XXXVI
XVII
VI

Answers:
22
36
17
6

ROMAN NUMERALS			
1	I	20	XX
2	II	30	XXX
3	III	40	XL
4	IV	50	L
5	V	60	LX
6	VI	70	LXX
7	VII	80	LXXX
8	VIII	90	XC
9	IX	100	C
10	X	500	D
		1000	M

St. Peter's Basilica
and its treasure!

Saint Peter's Basilica is the world's largest church. It is famous for its magnificence! A legend says it was built where **St. Peter** was buried. He was the first disciple, or follower, of Jesus Christ.

The Basilica is in **Vatican City** — the miniature state inside Rome. It's the home of the Pope, who is the head of the Roman Catholic Church.

What is the first thing you need to do when you get to St. Peter's Basilica?
Well ... you need to pass through St. Peter's **Square.** This huge space was built by the famous architect Bernini. It is bordered by grand colonnades (rows of columns). They are meant to symbolize a big embrace for all the people of the world.

What is located in the center of the square?

- A lion
- An obelisk
- The seat of the Pope

Answer: A lion

Can you guess how many statues of saints and martyrs stand on top of the colonnades?

How big is the Vatican City? Only 0.44 square km (0.17 square miles).

Answer: 140 statues

Help Leonardo find the Pope's window!

Every Sunday **from this window**, the Pope gives his welcome to the crowd that comes to St. Peter's Square. It is the second window from the right on the top floor ... Find it and take a picture!

St. Peter's Basilica — let's go inside!

And what's inside the Basilica?
The Basilica is decorated with beautiful monuments that show the power of the Catholic Church. The most famous one is the *Pietà*. It's a sculpture carved in marble by **Michelangelo.** It shows Mary's sorrow as she holds the dead body of Jesus.
This is the only statue by Michelangelo that has his signature.

Michelangelo is one of greatest artists of all times. He was born in Tuscany on March 6, 1475, but he spent most of his life in Rome. He worked as an architect, painter, and sculptor for Pope Julius II. Michelangelo showed great talent even when he was very young!

Can you find this famous statue by Michelangelo? It's near the entrance of the Basilica. Usually, you'll find many people gathered around the statue. Some people make drawings of it.

MICHELANGELO and the Sistine Chapel

Michelangelo is the creator of the majestic dome on **St. Peter's Basilica.**
It's huge — 42.34 meters (or almost 140 feet)!
Do you remember when Leonardo told you about great places to view the whole city? Well, this is one of the places!!!

The Sistine Chapel is the most famous sight in the Vatican Museum. You'll find it at the end of the Museum tour.

Did you know?
The chapel is named for Pope Sixtus IV. He had the chapel built in the 15th century AD.

Leonardo has discovered some big numbers for the Sistine Chapel:

- About 25,000 people a day, or 5 million people a year, visit the chapel.

- The chapel's paintings cover 1,110 square meters (12,000 square feet).

- Over 300 figures are painted on the chapel's ceiling.

What is the important event that still takes place in **the Sistine Chapel?**

When the **Pope** dies or retires, the Cardinals from all over the world come here to choose a new Pope. At a special meeting called a "conclave," every Cardinal casts his secret vote. They keep voting until someone gets enough votes to be the new Pope.
After every vote, either black or white smoke is sent up the chimney. The color lets people know whether a new Pope has been elected or not.
What color of smoke **announces the election of the new Pope?** Black or white?

Answer: White

Inside the Sistine Chapel

Look at the beautiful frescoes* painted on the walls and ceiling of the Sistine Chapel. Famous artists like Botticelli did the paintings on the walls. But the scenes on the ceiling are the most impressive and well-known. Michelangelo painted them in 1508.

*Fresco means "fresh" in Italian. The artist paints directly on the fresh, wet plaster of a wall.

Painting a fresco is very difficult. Can you think why? The painter has to complete the work before the paint dries ... and no mistakes are allowed. Otherwise, the artist has to start over from the beginning! 😟

Did you know?
Michelangelo liked sculpting more than anything. In the beginning, he didn't want to paint the Sistine Chapel. He only did it because Pope Julius II forced him to.

The Sistine Chapel's frescoes describe nine stories from the Christian Bible's book of Genesis.

Leonardo suggests that you use a mirror to see the ceiling better without hurting your neck! 😉

Can you find the most famous painting in the center of the ceiling?

It shows the most important moment, **the creation of Adam,** the first man created by God!

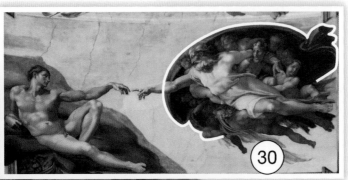

Leonardo suggests you look at this painting carefully. Can you find a brain in *The Creation of Adam* scene? Where?

Trevi Fountain ...

see the King of the Sea

Trevi Fountain (*Fontana di Trevi*) is the largest and most famous **baroque** fountain in Italy.

What is "baroque"?

Baroque art is very fancy and elaborate, with lots of ornaments. It was very popular In Europe in the 17th century. In Rome, you'll find lots of statues and fountains in the baroque style. Do you want to impress your family? Leonardo will help you recognize this style so you can tell your family what they are viewing!

Trevi Fountain is located at the end of the ancient aqueduct, or channel, called Aqua Virgo. It provided water for the thermal (hot) baths. The baths were very popular in ancient Rome ... kind of like swimming pools are today!

Guess how big **Trevi Fountain** is!

A - 25.9 meters high and 19.8 meters wide (about 85 feet high and 65 feet wide)
B - 200 meters high and 1 meter wide (about 656 feet high and 3-1/4 feet wide)
C - 1 meter high and 300 meters wide (3-1/4 feet high and 984 feet wide)

Answer: A - 25.9 meters high and 19.8 meters wide (about 85 feet high and 65 feet wide)

So what do you see ...? Discover the fountain with Leonardo and choose the right answers!
In the center is a big statue representing the King of the Sea:
- Oceanus
- Spiderman
- Superman

He is riding a chariot in the shape of a shell. On either side of him there is a triton (a sea god or goddess) and a
- Turtle
- Butterfly
- Horse

Answers: Horse Oceanus

Trevi Fountain ...
make a wish!

Have you heard of Neptune? He came after Oceanus, and he was called the God of the Sea. Can you see an important difference between Oceanus and Neptune? Leonardo suggests you look carefully at the two of them below! What is the difference?

Answer: Neptune is holding a three-pronged spear called a "trident."

Quizzes!

Leonardo wondered ... What do the Colosseum and Trevi Fountain have in common? Do you know the answer?

Answer: They were built with the same type of marble!

Find a nice place to sit with your family and color the picture of Neptune.

Did you know?

A legend says that if you throw a coin into Trevi Fountain, you are sure to come back to Rome. More than 3,000 euros (or over $4,000 US dollars) in coins are tossed into the fountain every day! 😨

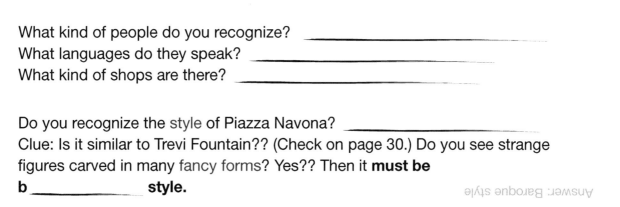

Piazza Navona
see Neptune's fountain and much more!

Welcome to **Piazza Navona!** Take a look around you.
What do you see in Piazza Navona?

What kind of people do you recognize? _____

What languages do they speak? _____

What kind of shops are there? _____

Do you recognize the style of Piazza Navona? _____
Clue: Is it similar to Trevi Fountain?? (Check on page 30.) Do you see strange figures carved in many fancy forms? Yes?? Then it **must be**
b _____ **style.**

Answer: Baroque style

Did you know?

Fights and chariot races were held in this square for many centuries.

In ancient Rome, going to chariot races was even more popular than watching gladiators! The chariots had two wheels and were pulled by horses. Some chariot drivers started training when they were just children. And many star drivers were teenagers.

You'll see Neptune with his trident in the fountain on the north side of the square. But you'll find the biggest fountain in the center of **Piazza Navona —** the Fountain of Four Rivers. Bernini built it. (He's the one who built St. Peter's Square!) It shows four major rivers: Nile I Ganges I Danube I Rio della Plata
They symbolize the four continents that were known at that time:
Africa I Asia I Europe I America

Do you know which river belongs to which continent?
Walk around the fountain, and help Leonardo find the river for each continent!

And what is in the center of the fountain?
• A lion
• Spiderman
• An obelisk

Answer: An obelisk

The Pantheon:
temple of all the gods

What does the word *pantheon* mean? It's Greek for "all the gods" (*pan*="all," *theon*="of the gods").

The Pantheon is a huge temple dedicated to all the Roman gods. It is the best-preserved monument in Rome! Emperor Hadrian had it built during the Roman Empire. But since 609 AD, it has been a Catholic church — the Basilica of St. Mary and the Martyrs.

Look up when you stand outside the Pantheon.

The triangle above the entrance is called a "pediment." It has a large sign; Leonardo tried to copy the words, but he missed a few letters. Can you help him complete the words?

M·A_RIP_A·L·F·_OS·TE_TI_M·FE_I_

What does it say? **It means** "Marcus Agrippa, son of Lucius, consul for the third time, built this." The sign remembers Marcus Agrippa, who created the first Pantheon in 27 BC. It was destroyed by a fire.

Help Leonardo describe the Pantheon by filling in the missing numbers: The entrance of the Pantheon is supported by _____ rows of enormous columns and giant bronze gates. **The first row has _____ columns and the other rows have _____ columns each.**

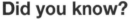

Answer:
• Three rows
• First row has eight columns
• The other rows have four columns each

Did you know?

The Pantheon's amazing dome is as high as it is wide. It is 43 meters (142 feet) from the floor to the top, and from one side to the other. It's the biggest unsupported concrete dome in the entire world!

Inside the Pantheon —
look up and see the sky!

The real wonder is its breathtaking dome!!
At the top of the dome, there is a hole — called the "oculus." It's open to the sky, and it lets light inside.

The oculus was never covered, so rain falls inside! But they had a smart idea! They built the floor to curve downward. That way, the rainwater could run off into small drains at the edges.

The huge space inside the dome is decorated with ancient sculptures and masterpieces by different artists.

Did you know?
The Pantheon is still used for weddings. And masses are celebrated there on important Catholic holy days.

Near the Pantheon, in the middle of the square, there is a fountain with an Egyptian obelisk. The obelisk was built by Pharaoh Ramses II. It was brought to Italy from the Temple of Ra in the Egyptian city of Heliopolis. Can you guess what style this fountain was built in? Think about the Trevi Fountain and Piazza Navona ... 😉

The SPANISH STEPS ... are you ready to start counting?

Welcome to the **Spanish Steps**, or as the Italians call it, *Piazza di Spagna*! It's the place where many Italians and tourists from all over the world come to meet each other!

This beautiful square is famous for **... its steps!**

You don't have to count them ... But Leonardo has counted all the steps to be sure of the right number. Guess how many?

A-40 steps   B-85 steps   C-135 steps   D-250 steps

Fill in the missing words:

The stairs connect the _____ (Square of Spagna) with _____, a baroque church.

Quizzes!

Why do you think it is called the Piazza di Spagna?

A - **Because** the Spanish people paid for this square

B - **Because** the Spanish Embassy is near Vatican City

C - **Because** a Spanish artist built the stairs

At the lower end of the stairs, you can find the Fountain of the Old Boat (or *Fontana della Barcaccia* in Italian). One legend says that after a huge flood of the Tiber River, a little boat was left on this exact spot! That was the inspiration for the fountain's statue!

Take a break at BioParco Zoo!

Do you want to take a break from seeing monuments, museums, and churches? Leonardo suggests visiting the BioParco Zoo!

Why?

This special zoo has more than 1,000 animals. There are 200 different species of mammals, birds, and reptiles. And most of the animals are in danger of becoming extinct. The BioParco Zoo tries to help the ones that are most at risk.

Follow the signposts located in the zoo! They show you how to find the animals you are looking for ... Be sure to see the King of the Jungle, the lion!

Tip!

You can also have a lot of fun at the recreation center: the Casina di Raffaello. Here you can find a wooden village, musical instruments, animal farm sculptures ... and so many other things to test your creativity!

Which animals **did you see** in the zoo?

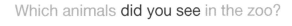

Did you see any special animals that you've **never seen before**?

_____

What is your **favorite animal** that lives in the BioParco Zoo?

_____

Family vote: What was the **most impressive thing** you saw in the zoo?

_____

Explora Museum: learning by doing!

Another good place to take a break — **the Explora Museum!**

This interactive museum was designed for kids. You can explore and learn in many different and fun ways. So let's go ... What do you prefer to be today?

- A scientist
- An astronaut
- A firefighter
- A TV news anchor
- Or _____

The museum has four areas:
- people
- communication
- environment
- society

Did you know?
Explora is the first museum in Italy created especially for kids! You can explore ecosystems, strange and interesting technology, and much more!

There are many fun rooms where you can play and learn. You can try being a doctor, a physicist, a scientist, a musician ... What areas did you visit? Write them here:

_____

Write about what you did:

_____

_____

Summary **of the trip**

We had great fun! What a pity it is over ....

How long did you stay in Rome?

_____

Where did you stay?

_____

What kinds of transportation did you use?

_____

Which places did you visit?

_____

_____

_____

What was each family member's favorite place?

_____ : _____

_____ : _____

_____ : _____

_____ : _____

Our family's most favorite place in Rome is:

_____

The souvenirs we bought in Rome were:

_____

The best food we ate in Rome was:

_____

Time for trivia!

Choose the right answer to the questions …

1. Who was Julius Caesar?
a. A Pope
b. An artist
c. A famous leader of ancient Rome

2. According to a legend, who founded the city of Rome?
a. A gladiator
b. Romulus and Remus
c. A wolf

3. People living in ancient Rome spoke this language:
a. English
b. Italian
c. Latin

4. What is a temple? A place where …
a. People play football
b. Gods are honored with worship and prayers
c. Animals can graze

5. What is the Colosseum?
a. A huge, ancient stadium in Rome
b. A modern stadium for playing football
c. A big column in the center of Rome

6. Where does the Pope live today?
a. In a museum
b. In Vatican City
c. In the Sistine Chapel

7. These letters mean the number "8" in Latin: VIII
a. True
b. False

8. What is the best-preserved monument in Rome?
a. The Pantheon
b. The BioParco Zoo
c. The Spanish Steps

9. Rome is the capital of Italy?
a. True
b. False

10. How many years did the Roman Empire last?
a. About 100 years
b. About 20 years
c. More than 400 years

11. Who were the gladiators?
a. Slaves forced to fight in stadiums like the Colosseum
b. The most courageous Roman soldiers
c. The Kings of Rome

12. Rome is built on four hills.
a. True
b. False

13. An ingredient in pizza is:
a. Grapes
b. Plain flour
c. Tortillas

14. How many rivers cross Rome?
a. 5
b. 1
c. None